Mrs. Mary Eales's Receipts
[1718]

reproduced from the
edition of 1733

PROSPECT BOOKS: LONDON
1985

This facsimile edition published in 1985
by Prospect Books Ltd
45 Lamont Road
London SW10 0HU

Distributed in the USA by
the University Press of Virginia

Designer Philip Wills

Added text set by Ronset, Darwen, Lancs
Printed and bound by
Smith Settle, Otley Mills, Otley, W Yorks

ISBN 0 907325 25 4

[redacted]

Introduction

Mrs Mary Eales, who styled herself 'Confectioner to her late Majesty Queen Anne' (1702–1714) wrote one book, called *Mrs. Mary Eales's Receipts*, which appeared in 1718 and had a curious publishing history.

Although the book was pleasantly specialized and well composed, and had the distinction of containing the first published English recipe for ice cream,[1] it was not reprinted in the author's lifetime. However, it reappeared in 1733, with slight differences in printers' ornaments and suchlike details, but otherwise unchanged. In the same year it was also published, 'with the Consent of her Executors' under a new title, *The Compleat Confectioner*. Again, the text was the same as that of 1718. The only significant differences were the changed title page and the addition of a two-page Advertisement explaining how rare the original work had become (but making no allusion to its also being reprinted under the original title in the same year).

No 2nd edition of *The Compleat Confectioner* is known, but copies exist of the 3rd edition, 1742. This book was twice as long. The original text was preserved, but followed by a second part of equal length. This added material, preceded by its own title page, was a hodge-podge of cookery (including some confectionery, but also 'Soops' and meat and fish dishes), pickling, medicinal receipts and brewing instructions. A 5th edition (1753) survives, but there seems to be no trace of a 4th.

Mrs Eales' legacy was next exploited in 1767,

when what was described as the 2nd edition of *Mrs. Mary Eales's Receipts* was published. It exhibited one change from the 1st edition and that of 1733, in that it included a 4-page Introduction on the stages of boiling sugar. Otherwise it was the same as its predecessors.

What appears to have been the last edition (until the present one) of Mrs Eales' work was published in about 1788. It was described as 'a new edition', comprising 'A New Collection of Receipts in Confectionary . . . Collected by Several Hands'; but it contained nothing new. It was simply a reprint, under the title *The Compleat Confectioner*, of the 1767 edition of *Mrs. Mary Eales's Receipts*, complete with the added pages on sugar boiling.

The bibliographies have not illuminated this peculiar progression as fully as they might have done.[2]

We have examined all versions of Mrs Eales' work.[3] It is abundantly clear that what deserves to be resuscitated is what she published in 1718. But from the copies available for inspection it seemed equally clear that this text would be reproduced with the most pleasing effect from the 1733 reprint, which was better executed. So that is the version we have used.

The exact status of Mrs Eales as 'Confectioner' to Queen Anne is something of a mystery.[4] Court documents preserved at the Public Record Office in London include the Account Books of the Lord Steward for all the years of Queen Anne's reign. These show there was a distinct department of the Royal Household whose responsibility was confectionery for the Court. Throughout the reign this was composed of three people: Elizabeth Stephens, George Gunthorpe, Thomas Drake. There is no mention in these records of Mrs Eales.

However, there is evidence which suggests that, although the Royal Confectioners were responsible for supplying the Court with confectionery, they often brought it in from outside. Elizabeth Stephens, George Gunthorpe, and Thomas Drake are all recorded as receiving payments for supplying confectionery to members of the Court and the Royal Family. In 1707, for example, the Book of Creditors, as the relevant document is known, records 35 shillings paid to 'Elizabeth Stephens Confectioner' for supplying in October '8lb of Quince Marmalade for His Royal Highness Breakfast at 4s. the 1b 32s. and Carraways for Her Majesty 3s. in all by her provided and delivered'. Elizabeth Stephens was a member of the household and as such received a regular salary; so this payment looks like reimbursement for outside purchases. Similar payments are recorded, frequently but irregularly, to both George Gunthorpe and Thomas Drake for 1707 and other years. No details of outside suppliers have come to light. However, on the strength of the claim made by Mrs Eales on her title page, it seems reasonable to suppose that it was she who made a good proportion of the confectionery which the official Confectioners supplied to the Court.

A Mary Eales is recorded on 6 March 1731 as having lately died in the Parish of St Leonard Shoreditch, Middlesex. She had left no will and the estate was granted to her only daughter, also called Mary Eales. The deceased lady could have been 'our' Mrs Eales. The date fits well enough with the sudden republication of her book under two different imprints in 1733.

Although little is known about Mrs Eales, her clear style bespeaks a woman who knew her job; and the limited scope of her book suggests that she stuck to what she knew. These virtues shine all the brighter for being rare.

NOTES

1. See 'Ice Cream and Water Ices in 17th and 18th century England' by W. S. Stallings Jr, a Supplement to *Petits Propos Culinaires*, no 3 (1979), p 3.

2. Oxford starts off with the original book of 1718; records the two reprints under different titles of 1733; mentions the 5th edition of *The Compleat Confectioner* (1753), but without any indication that it had acquired a second part and doubled in size; and otherwise mentions only the 1767 edition of *Mrs. Mary Eales's Receipts*, 'corrected, with additions' (additions which he does not specify). The reader is left with the impression that there was really only one book (although two titles) and that the only changes occurred in 1767. It is indeed correct that Mrs Eales only wrote one book; but it is misleading not to mention the considerable accretion which was foisted onto it under its later alternative title.

Bitting quotes Oxford and adds a brief indication that the edition of 1742 contains added matter in the form of recipes for things other than confectionery, including brewing, but gives little idea of the extent of this added matter.

Maclean, writing of *Mrs. Mary Eales's Receipts* (edition of 1718), states: 'Although this work by Mary Eales bears great similarity to her later published work, The Compleat Confectioner . . ., there are sufficient differences to allow them to be regarded as separate books.' Not so, up to and including 1733. Later on, however, the differences, involving a doubling in size of one version, were certainly sufficient to justify separate treatment.

3. Jennifer Stead undertook this task at the Brotherton Library of the University of Leeds.

4. Marcus Bell carried out the research on which this and the following two paragraphs are based.

Mrs. Mary Eales's Receipts
[1718]

Mrs. *Mary Eales's*

RECEIPTS.

CONFECTIONER to her late MAJESTY Queen *ANNE.*

L O N D O N:

Printed for J. BRINDLEY, Bookseller, at the *King's-Arms* in *New Bond-Street*, and Bookbinder to Her Majesty and His Royal Highness the Prince of *Wales*; and R. MONTAGU at the *General Post-Office*, the Corner of *Great Queen-Street*, near *Drury-Lane*.
MDCCXXXIII.

THE

CONTENTS.

To dry Angelica	Page 1
To preserve green Apricocks	2
To make Goosberry Clear-Cakes	3
To make Goosberry-Paste	4
To dry Goosberries	5
To preserve Goosberries	6
To dry Cherries	7
To make Cherry-Jam	8
To dry Cherries without Sugar	ibid.
To dry Cherries in Bunches	9
To make Cherry-Paste	ib.
To preserve Cherries	10
To dry Currants in Bunches, &c.	11
To make Currant Clear-Cakes	12
To preserve red Currants	13
To make Currant Paste, either red or white	ib.

The CONTENTS.

To preserve white Currants Page 14
To preserve Rasberries 15
To make Jam of Rasberries 16
To make Rasberry-Paste ib.
To make Rasberry Clear-Cakes 17
To make Rasberry-Drops 18
To dry Apricocks ib.
To dry Apricocks in Quarters or Halves 19
To make Paring-Chips 20
To preserve Apricocks 21
To make Apricock Clear-Cakes 22
To make Apricock-Paste 23
To make Apple-Jelly for all Sorts of Sweet-Meats ib.
To make Apricock-Jam 24
To preserve green Jennitins ib.
To dry green Plums 25
To dry Amber, or any white Plums 26
To dry black Pear-Plums, or Muscles, or the Great Moguls 28
To preserve black Pear-Plums or Damascenes 30
To preserve white Pear-Plums ib.
To make white Pear-Plum Clear-Cakes 31
To make white Plum-Paste 32
To make red Plum Clear-Cakes 33
To make red Plum-Paste 34
To dry Plums like the French *Plums, with Stones in them* ib.

To

The CONTENTS.

To dry Peaches Page 35
To make Peach-Chips 36
To preserve or dry Nutmeg-Peaches 37
To preserve Cucumbers ib.
To dry green Figs 39
To dry black Figs 40
To preserve Grapes 41
To dry Grapes ib.
To dry Barberries 42
To preserve Barberries 43
To make Barberry-Drops ib.
To make white Quince-Marmalet 44
To make red Quince-Marmalet 45
To preserve whole Quinces 46
To make Quince-Chips 47
To make Quince-Paste 48
To make Quince Clear-Cakes ib.
To preserve Golden or Kentish-*Pippins* 49
To preserve whole Oranges or Lemmons 50
To dry Oranges in Knots, or Lemmons 52
To make China-*Chips* 54
To make Orange-Paste ib.
To make Orange-Drops 55
To make Orange-Marmalet 56
To make Orange or Lemmon Clear-Cakes ib.
To make Pomegranate Clear-Cakes 58
To make Orange-Halves, or Quarters, with the Meat in them 59
To preserve Citrons. 60

To

The CONTENTS.

To make Citron-Marmalet Page 61
To candy Orange-Flowers ib.
To make Rock-Sugar 63
To make Fruit-Biſcuit 65
To make all Sorts of Sugar-Paſte 66
To make Chocolate-Almonds 67
To make Wormwood-Cakes ib.
To make Honycomb-Cakes of Orange-Flower-Violet of Cowſlips 68
To make Ice Almond-Cakes ib.
To make Bean'd-Bread 69
To make Orange or Lemmon-Puffs 70
To make Almond-Paſte, either Bitter or Sweet 71
To make little round Ratafea-Puffs 72
To make Brown Wafers ib.
To make Almond-Loaves 73
To make Chocolate-Puffs 74
To make Ratafea-Drops, either of Apricock-Kernels, or half Bitter and half Sweet-Almonds ib.
To make all Sorts of Sugar-Puffs 75
To make Almond-Paſte ib.
To make long Biſcuit 76
To make Spunge-Biſcuit 77
To make round Biſcuit with Coriander-Seeds 78
To make Hartſhorn-Jelly 79
To make Lemmon-Jelly ib.

To

To make Butter'd Orange Page 80
To make Eringo-Cream ib.
To make Barley-Cream 81
To make Ratafea-Cream ib.
To make Almond-Butter 82
To make a Trifle ib.
To make all Sorts of Fruit-Cream 83
To make Sack-Poſſet, or Sack-Cream ib.
To make Blamange 84
Lemmon-Cream, made with Cream 85
To make Citron-Cream ib
To make Piſtato-Cream 86
To make Clouted-Cream ib.
To make a very thick, raw Cream 87
To make Spaniſh-*Butter* ib.
To make Orange-Butter 88
To make Almond-Butter 89
To make Trout-Cream ib.
To make Almond-Cream 90
To make Raw-Almond, or Ratafea-Cream 91
To make Chocolate-Cream ib.
To make Sego-Cream 92
To ice Cream ib.
To make Hartſhorn-Flummery 93
To make perfum'd Paſtels 94
To burn Almonds 95
To make Lemmon-Wafers ib.
To candy little green Oranges 97

To candy Cowſlips, or any Flowers or Greens, in Bunches ib.
To make Caramel 98
To make a good Green 99
To Sugar all Sorts of ſmall Fruit ib.
To ſcald all Sorts of Fruit 100

Mrs. *EALES*'s

RECEIPTS.

To dry ANGELICA.

TAKE the Stalks of Angelica, and boil them tender; then put them to drain, and ſcrape off all the thin Skin, and put them into ſcalding Water; keep them cloſe cover'd, and over a ſlow Fire, not to boil, 'till they are green; then draining them well, put them in a very thick Syrup of the Weight and half of Sugar: Let the Syrup be cold when you put them in, and warm it every Day 'till it is clear, when you may lay them out to dry, ſifting Sugar upon them. Lay out but as much as you uſe at a Time, and ſcald the reſt.

To preſerve green APRICOCKS.

TAKE Apricocks before the Stones are very hard; wet them, and lay them in a coarſe Cloth; put to them two or three large Handfuls of Salt, rub them 'till the Roughneſs is off, then put them in ſcalding Water; ſet them over the Fire 'till they almoſt boil, then ſet them off the Fire 'till they are almoſt cold; do ſo two or three Times; after this, let them be cloſe cover'd; and when they look to be green, let them boil 'till they begin to be tender weigh them, and make a Syrup of their Weight in Sugar, to a Pound of Sugar allowing half a Pint of Water to make the Syrup; let it be almoſt cold before you put in the Apricocks; boil them up well 'till they are clear; warm the Syrup daily, 'till it is pretty thick. You may put them in a Codling-

Jelly,

Jelly, or Hartſhorn Jelly, or dry them as you uſe them.

To make Goosberry CLEAR-CAKES.

TAKE a Gallon of white Gooſberries, noſe and waſh them; put to them as much Water as will cover them almoſt all over, ſet them on an hot Fire, let them boil a Quarter of an Hour, or more, then run it thro' a Flannel Jelly-Bag; to a Pint of Jelly have ready a Pound and half of fine Sugar, ſifted thro' an Hair Sieve; ſet the Jelly over the Fire, let it juſt boil up, then ſhake in the Sugar, ſtirring it all the while the Sugar is putting in; then ſet it on the Fire again, let it ſcald 'till all the Sugar is well melted; then lay a thin Strainer in a flat earthen Pan, pour in your Clear-Cake Jelly, and turn back the Strainer to take off the Scum; fill it into Pots, and ſet it in the Stove to dry; when it is candy'd on the Top, turn it out on Glaſs; and if your Pots are too big, cut it; and when it is very dry, turn it again, and let it dry on the other Side; twice turning is enough. If any of the Cakes ſtick to the Glaſs, hold them over a little Fire, and they will come off: Take Care the Jelly does not boil after the Sugar is in: A Gallon of Gooſberries will make three Pints of Jelly; if more, 'twill not be ſtrong enough.

To make GOOSBERRY-PASTE.

TAKE the Gooſberries, noſe and waſh them, put to them as much Water as will almoſt cover them, and let them boil a Quarter of an Hour; then ſtrain them thro' a thin Strainer, or an Hair-Sieve, and allow to a Pint of Liquor a Pound and half of fine Sugar, ſifted thro' a Hair-Sieve; before you put in the Sugar, ſet the Liquor on the Fire, let it boil, and ſcum it; then ſhake in the Sugar, ſet it on the Fire again, and let it ſcald 'till all the Sugar is melted; then fill it into little Pots; when it is candy'd, turn it out on Glaſs; and when it is dry on one Side,

Side, turn it again; if any of the Cakes ſtick, hold the Glaſs over the Fire: You may put ſome of this in Plates; and when it is jelly'd, before it candies, cut it out in long Slices, and make Fruit-Jambals.

To dry GOOSBERRIES.

TAKE the large white Gooſberries before they are very ripe, but at full Growth, ſtone and waſh them, and to a Pound of Gooſberries put a Pound and half of Sugar, beat very fine, and half a Pint of Water; ſet them on the Fire; when the Sugar is melted, let them boil, but not too faſt; take them off once or twice, that they may not break; when they begin to look clear, they are enough: Let them ſtand all Night in the Pan they are boil'd in, with a Paper laid cloſe to them; the next Day ſcald them very well, and let them ſtand a Day or two; then lay them on Plates, ſift them with Sugar very well, and put them in the Stove, turning them every Day 'till they

are

are dry; the third Time of turning, you may lay them on a Sieve, if you pleaſe; when they are pretty dry, place them in a Box, with Paper betwixt every Row.

To preſerve GOOSBERRIES.

TAKE the white Gooſberries, ſtamp and ſtrain them; then take the largeſt white Gooſberries when they juſt begin to turn, ſtone them, and to half a Pound of the Gooſberries put a Pound of Loaf Sugar beaten very fine, half a Pint of the Juice of that which is ſtrain'd, (but let it ſtand 'till it is ſettled and very clear) and ſix Spoonfuls of Water; ſet them on a very quick Fire; let them boil as faſt as you can make them, up to the Top of the Pan; when you ſee the Sugar as it boils look clear, they are enough, which will be in leſs than half a quarter of an Hour: Put them in Pots or Glaſſes, paper them cloſe; the next Day, if they are not hard enough jelly'd, ſet them for a Day or two on an hot Stove, or in ſome warm Place, but not in in the Sun; and when they are jelly'd, put Papers cloſe to 'em; the Papers muſt be firſt wet, and then dry'd with a Cloth.

To dry CHERRIES.

STONE the Cherries; and to ten Pound of Cherries, when they are ſton'd, put three Pound of Sugar very fine beaten; ſhake the Cherries and Sugar well together, ſet them on the Fire, and when the Sugar is well melted, give them a Boil or two; let them ſtand in an earthen Pot 'till the next Day, then make them ſcalding hot, and, when cold, lay them on Sieves; afterwards put them in an Oven not too hot, where let them ſtand all Night, and then turn them, and put them in again. Let your Oven be no hotter than it is after ſmall Bread or Pies. When they are dry, keep them in a Box very cloſe, with no Paper between them.

To

To make CHERRY-JAM.

TAKE twelve Pound of ſton'd Cherries, boil them, break them as they boil; and when you have boiled all the Juice away, and can ſee the Bottom of the Pan, put in three Pound of Sugar finely beaten, ſtir it well, and let them have two or three Boils; then put them in Pots or Glaſſes.

To dry CHERRIES *without Sugar.*

STONE the Cherries, and ſet them on the Fire, with only what Liquor comes out of them; let them boil up two or three Times, ſhaking them as they boil; then put them in an earthen Pot; the next Day ſcald them, and when they are cold lay them on Sieves, and dry them in an Oven not too hot. Twice heating an Oven will dry any Sort of Cherries.

To dry CHERRIES *in Bunches.*

TAKE *Kentish* Cherries, or *Morella*, and tye them in Bunches with a Thread, about a Dozen in a Bunch; and when you have dry'd your other Cherries, put the Syrup that they come out of to your Bunches; let them juſt boil, cover them cloſe, the next Day ſcald them; and when they are cold, lay them in Sieves in a cool Oven; turn them, and heat the Oven every Day 'till they are dry.

To make CHERRY-PASTE.

TAKE Cherries, ſtone and boil them, breaking them well the while, and boil them very dry; and to a Pound of Cherries put a Pound and a Quarter of Sugar, ſifted thro' an Hair Sieve; let the Cherries be hot when you put in the Sugar; ſet it on the Fire 'till the Sugar is well melted; put it in a broad Pan, or earthen Plates; let it ſtand in the Stove 'till it is candy'd; drop it on Glaſs, and, when dry on one Side, turn it.

To preſerve CHERRIES.

EITHER *Morella* or *Carnations*, ſtone the Cherries: To *Morella* Cherries, take the Jelly of white Currants, drawn with a little Water; and run thro a Jelly-bag a Pint and a half of the Jelly, and three Pounds of fine Sugar; ſet it on a quick Fire; when it boils, ſcum it, and put in two Pounds of the ſton'd Cherries; let them not boil too faſt at firſt, take them off ſome Times; when they are tender, boil them very faſt 'till they jelly, and are very clear; then put them in the Pots or Glaſſes. The *Carnation* Cherries muſt have red Currants-Jelly; and if you can get no white Currants, Codling-Jelly will ſerve for the *Morella*.

To dry CURRANTS *in Bunches or loose Sprigs.*

WHEN your Currants are ſton'd and ty'd up in Bunches, take to a Pound of Currants a Pound and half of Sugar; to a Pound of Sugar put half a Pint of Water; boil your Syrup very well, and lay the Currants into the Syrup; ſet them on the Fire, let them juſt boil, take them off, and cover them cloſe with a Paper; let them ſtand 'till the next Day, and then make them ſcalding hot; let them ſtand two or three Days with the Paper cloſe to them; then lay them on earthen Plates, and ſift them well with Sugar; put them into a Stove; the next Day lay them on Sieves, but not turn them 'till that Side drys, then turn them, and ſift the other Side: When they are dry lay them between Papers.

To make CURRANT CLEAR-CAKES.

STRIP the Currants, waſh them, and to a Gallon of Currants put about a Quart of Water; boil it very well, run it thro' a Jelly-bag; to a Pint of Jelly put a Pound and half of Sugar, ſifted thro' an Hair Sieve; ſet your Jelly on the Fire, let it juſt boil; then ſhake in the Sugar, ſtir it well, ſet it on the Fire, and make it ſcalding hot; then put it thro' a Strainer in a broad Pan, to take off the Scum, and fill it in Pots: When it is candy'd, turn it on Glaſs 'till that Side be dry; then turn it again, to dry on the other Side.

Red and white Currants are done the ſame Way; but as ſoon as the Jelly of the White is made, you muſt put it to the Sugar, or it will change Colour.

To preserve RED CURRANTS.

MASH the Currants, and ſtrain them thro' a thin Strainer; take a Pint of Juice, a Pound and half of Sugar, and ſix Spoonfuls of Water; let it boil up, and ſcum it very well; then put in half a Pound of ſton'd Currants; boil them as faſt as you can, 'till the Currants are clear and jelly very well; put them in Pots or Glaſſes, and, when they are cold, paper them as other Sweet-meats. Stir all ſmall Fruit as they cool, to mix it with the Jelly.

To make CURRANT-PASTE, *either Red or White.*

STRIP the Currants, and put a little Water to them, juſt to keep them from ſticking to the Pan; boil them well, and rub them thro' a Hair Sieve: To a Pint of Juice put a Pound and a half of Sugar ſifted; but firſt boil the Juice after it is ſtrain'd, ſtrain'd, and then ſhake in your Sugar: Let it ſcald 'till the Sugar is melted; then put it in little Pots in a Stove, and turn it as other Paſte.

To preſerve WHITE CURRANTS.

TAKE the large white Currants, not the Amber-colour'd, ſtrip them, and to two Quarts of Currants put a Pint of Water; boil them very faſt, and run them thro' a Jelly-bag; to a Pint of Juice put in a Pound and half of Sugar, and half a Pound of ſton'd Currants; ſet them on a quick Fire, let them boil very faſt, 'till the Currants are clear and jelly very well; then put them in Pots or Glaſſes; ſtir them as they cool, to make the Currants mix with the Jelly: Paper them down when almoſt cold.

To preserve RASBERRIES.

TAKE the Juice of red and white Raſberries; (if you have no white Raſberries, uſe half Codling-Jelly) put a Pint and half of the Juice to two Pound of Sugar; let it boil, ſcum it, and then put in three Quarters of a Pound of large Raſberries; let them boil very faſt, 'till they jelly and are very clear; don't take them off the Fire, for that will make them hard; a Quarter of an Hour will do them. after they begin to boil faſt; then put them in Pots or Glaſſes: Put the Raſberries in firſt, then ſtrain the Jelly from the Seeds, and put it to the Raſberries. When they begin to cool, ſtir them, that they may not all lye upon the Top of the Glaſſes; and when they are cold, lay Papers cloſe to them; firſt wet the Paper, then dry it in a Cloth.

To make JAM *of* RASBERRIES.

TAKE the Raſberries, maſh them, and ſtrain half; put the Juice to the other half that has the Seeds in it; boil it faſt for a Quarter of an Hour; then to a Pint of Raſberries put three Quarters of a Pound of Sugar, and boil it 'till it jellies: Put it into Pots or Glaſſes.

To make RASBERRY-PASTE.

MASH the Raſberries, ſtrain half, and put the Juice to the other half with the Seeds; boil them faſt for a Quarter of an Hour; and to a Pint of Raſberries put half a Pint of red Currants, boil'd with very little Water, and ſtrain'd thro' a thin Strainer, or Hair Sieve; let the Currants and Raſberries boil together a little while: Then to a Pint of Juice put a Pound and a Quarter of ſifted Sugar; ſet it over the Fire, let it ſcald, but not boil;

fill

fill it in little Pots, ſet it in the Stove 'till it is candy'd, then turn it out on Glaſſes, as other Cakes.

To make RASBERRY CLEAR-CAKES.

TAKE half Raſberries and half white Currants, almoſt cover them with Water; boil them very well a Quarter of an Hour, then run them thro' a Jelly-bag, and to every Pint of Jelly have ready a Pound and half of fine Sugar, ſifted thro' an Hair Sieve; ſet the Jelly on the Fire, let it juſt boil, then ſhake in your Sugar, ſtir it well, and ſet it on the Fire a ſecond Time, 'till the Sugar is melted; then lay a Strainer in a broad Pan to prevent the Scum, and fill it into Pots: When it is candy'd, turn it on Glaſs, as other Clear-Cakes.

To make Rasberry-Drops.

MASH the Rasberries, put in a little Water, boil and strain them, then take half a Pound of fine Sugar, sifted thro' an Hair Sieve; just wet the Sugar to make it as thick as a Paste; put to it twenty Drops of Spirits of Vitriol, set it over the Fire, making it scalding hot, but not to boil: Drop it on Paper it will soon be dry; if it will not come off easily, wet the Paper. Let them lye a Day or two on the Paper.

To dry Apricocks.

TAKE four Dozen and a half of the largest Apricocks, stone them and pare them; cover them all over with four Pound of Sugar finely beaten; put some of the Sugar on them as you pare them, the rest after: Let them lye four or five Hours, 'till the Sugar is almost melted; then set them on a slow Fire 'till quite melted; then boil them,

but

but not too faſt. As they grow tender, take them out on an earthen Plate 'till the reſt are done; then put in thoſe that you laid out firſt, and let them have a Boil together: Put a Paper cloſe to them, and let them ſtand a Day or two; then make them very hot, but not boil; put the Paper on them as before, and let them ſtand two Days, then lay them on earthen Plates in a Stove, with as little Syrup on them as you can; turn them every Day 'till they are dry, and ſcrape off the Syrup as you turn them; lay them between Paper, and let them not be too dry before you lay them up.

To dry APRICOCKS *in Quarters or Halves.*

TAKE four Pound of the Halves or Quarters, pare them, and put to them three Pound of Sugar fine beaten; ſtrew ſome on them as you pare them, and cover them with the reſt; let them lye four or five Hours; afterwards ſet them on a ſlow Fire, till the Sugar is melted; then boil them, but not too faſt, 'till they are tender, taking out thoſe that are firſt tender; and putting them in again, let them have a Boil together; then lay a Paper cloſe to them, ſcald them very well, and let them lye a Day or two in the Syrup: Lay them on earthen Plates, with as little Syrup to them as you can, turning them every Day 'till they are dry; at laſt, lay them between Paper in Boxes.

To make PARING-CHIPS.

AS you pare your Apricocks, ſave the cleareſt Parings, and throw a little Sugar on them; half a Pound is ſufficient to a Pound of the Parings; ſet them on the Fire, let them juſt boil up, and ſet them by 'till the next Day; drain the Syrup from them, and make a Syrup with a Pound of Sugar and almoſt half a Pint of Water; boil the Sugar very well, and put as much to the Chips when it is cold as will cover them; let them ſtand in the Syrup all Night, and the next Day make them ſcalding hot; and when they are cold,

cold, lay them out on Boards, ſift them with Sugar, and turn them on Sieves.

To preſerve APRICOCRS.

TAKE four Dozen of large Apricocks, ſtone and pare them, and cover them with three Pound of fine beaten Sugar, ſtrewing ſome on as you pare them; let them ſtand, at leaſt, ſix or ſeven Hours, then boil them on a ſlow Fire 'till they are clear and tender; if ſome of them are clear before the reſt, take them out, and put them in again when the reſt are ready. Let them ſtand, with a Paper cloſe to them, 'till the next Day; then make Codling-Jelly very ſtrong: Take two Pints of Jelly, two Pound of Sugar, boil it 'till it jellies; and whilſt it is boiling, make your Apricocks ſcalding hot, and put the Jelly to your Apricocks, and boil them together, but not too faſt. When the Apricocks riſe in the Jelly, and they jelly very well, put them into Pots or Glaſſes, with Papers cloſe to them.

To

To make APRICOCK CLEAR-CAKES.

TAKE about three Dozen of Apricocks, pare them, and put thereto a Pound of fine Sugar, and boil them to Pieces; then put to them two Quarts of Codling-Jelly, boil them together very faſt for a Quarter of an Hour; run it thro' a Jelly-bag, and to a Pint of Jelly put a Pound and half of Sugar, ſifted thro' a Hair Sieve; while the Jelly boils, ſhake in your Sugar, and let it ſcald 'till the Sugar is melted; then put it thro' a thin Strainer, in a broad earthen Pan; fill it in Pots, and dry it as other Clear-Cakes. If you would have ſome with Pieces in them, cut ſome of your dry'd Quarters ſmall; and when the Strainer has taken off the Scum, take ſome of the Jelly in a Pan, put in the Pieces, make it ſcalding hot again, and fill it out.

To

To make APRICOCK-PASTE.

TAKE two Pound of Apricocks par'd, and a Pound of Sugar fine beaten, let them lye in the Sugar 'till it is melted; then boil it well and maſh it very ſmall; put to it two Pints of Codling-Jelly; let it boil together; and to a Pound of it put a Pound and a Quarter of ſifted Sugar; let your Paſte boil before you put your Sugar to it, then let it ſcald 'till the Sugar is melted; fill it in Pots, and dry it in the Stove, turning it as other Paſte.

To make APPLE-JELLY *for all Sorts of* SWEET-MEATS.

LET your Water boil in the Pan you make it in; and when the Apples are par'd and quarter'd, put them into the boiling Water; let there be no more Water than juſt to cover them, and let it boil as faſt as poſſible; when the Apples are all to Pieces, put in about a Quart of Water more; let

it

it boil at leaſt half an Hour; and then run it thro' a Jelly-bag: In the *Summer*, Codlings are beſt; in *September*, Golden Runnets and *Winter* Pippins.

To make APRICOCK-JAM.

TAKE two Pound of Apricocks par'd, and a Pint of Codling-Jelly, boil them very faſt together 'till the Jelly is almoſt waſted; then put to it a Pound and half of fine Sugar, and boil it very faſt 'till it jellies; put it into Pots or Glaſſes. You may make freſh Clear-Cakes with this, and Pippin-Jelly, in the *Winter*.

To preſerve GREEN JENNITINS.

CUT out the Stalk and Noſe, and put them in cold Water on a Coal-Fire 'till they peel; then put them in the ſame Water, and cover them very cloſe; ſet them on a ſlow Fire 'till they are green and tender; then, to a Pound

Pound of Apples take a Pound and half of Sugar, and half a Pint of Water; boil the Syrup, put in the Apples, and boil them faſt, 'till they are very clear, and the Syrup very thick, almoſt at a Candy; then put in half a Pint, or more, of Codling-Jelly, and the Juice of a Lemon, boil it 'till it jellies well, and put them in Pots or Glaſſes.

To dry GREEN PLUMS.

TAKE the green Amber Plum, prick it all over with a Pin; make Water boiling hot, and put in the Plums, be ſure you have ſo much Water, that it be not cold with the Plums going in; cover them very cloſe, and when they are almoſt cold, ſet them on the Fire again, but not to let them boil; do ſo three or four Times; when you ſee the thin Skin crack'd, fling in a Handful of Allum fine beaten, and keep them in a Scald 'till they begin to be green, then give them a Boil cloſe cover'd: When they are green, let them ſtand all Night in freſh hot Water; the next Day have ready as much clarify'd Sugar as will cover them; drain your Plums, put them into the Syrup, and give them two or three Boils; repeat it two or three Days, 'till they are very clear; let them ſtand in their Syrup above a Week; then lay them out on Sieves, in a hot Stove, to dry: If you would have your Plums green very ſoon, inſtead of Allom, take Verdigreece finely beaten, and put in Vinegar; ſhake it in a Bottle, and put it into them when the Skin cracks; let them have a Boil, and they will be very ſoon green; you may put ſome of them in Codling-Jelly, firſt boiling the Jelly with the Weight in Sugar.

To dry AMBER, *or any* WHITE PLUMS.

SLIT your Plums in the Seam; then make a thin Syrup. If you have any Apricock-Syrup left, after your Apricocks are dry'd, put a Pint of Syrup to two Quarts of Water; if you

you have none, clarify ſingle-refin'd Loaf-Sugar, and make a thin Syrup: Make the Syrup ſcalding hot, and put in the Plums; there muſt be ſo much Syrup as will more than cover the Plums; they muſt be kept under the Syrup, or they will turn red: Keep them in a Scald 'till they are tender, but not too ſoft; then have ready a thick Syrup of the ſame Sugar, clarify'd and cold, as much as will cover the Plums; let them boil, but not too faſt, 'till they are very tender and clear, ſetting them ſometimes off the Fire; then lay a Paper cloſe to them, and ſet them by 'till the next Day; then boil them again 'till the Syrup is very thick; let them lye in the Syrup four or five Days, then lay them on Sieves to dry: You may put ſome in Codling-Jelly, firſt boiling the Jelly with the Weight in Sugar, and put in the Plums hot to the Jelly. Put them in Pots or Glaſſes.

To dry BLACK PEAR-PLUMS, *or* MUSCLES, *or the* GREAT MOGULS.

STONE your Plums, and put them in a large earthen Pot; make a Syrup with a Pound of ſingle-refin'd Sugar and three Pints of Water; or if you have the Syrup the white Plums are dry'd out of, thin it with Water, it will do as well as Sugar; boil your Syrup well, and when it is cold enough to hold your Hand in it, put it to the Plums; cover them cloſe, and let them ſtand all Night; heat the Syrup two or three Times, but never too hot; when they are tender, lay them on Sieves, with the Slit downwards to dry; put them in the Oven, made no hotter than it is after Bread or Pyes come out of it; let them ſtand all Night therein; then open them and turn them, and ſet them in a cool Oven again, or in an hot Stove, for a Day or two; but if they are too dry, they will not be ſmooth; then make a Jam to fill them with. Take ten Pound of Plums, the ſame Sort of your Skins, cut them off the Stones,

put

put to them three Pound of Powder-Sugar; boil them on a ſlow Fire, keeping them ſtirring 'till it's ſo ſtiff, that it will lye in a Heap in the Pan; it will be boiling at leaſt four or five Hours; lay it on Earthen Plates; when it is cold, break it with your Hands, and fill your Skins; then waſh every Plum, and wipe all the Clam off with a Cloth: As you waſh them, lay them on a Sieve; put them in the Oven, make your Oven as hot as for your Skins; let them ſtand all Night, and they will be blue in the Morning. The great white Mogul makes a fine black Plum; ſtone them, and put them in the Syrup with or after the black Plum; and heat the Syrup every Day, 'till they are of a dark Colour; they will blue as well as the Muſcles, and better than the black Pear-Plums. If any of theſe Plums grow ruſty in the *Winter*, put them into boiling hot Water; let them lye no longer than to be well waſh'd: Lay them on a Sieve, not ſingly, but one on the other, and they will blue the better: Put them in a cool Oven all Night, they will be as blue and freſh as at firſt.

To preserve Black Pear-Plums or Damascenes.

TAKE two Pound of Plums, and cut them in the Seam; then take a Pint and half of Jelly, made of the ſame Plum, and three Pound and a half of Sugar; boil the Jelly and Sugar, and ſcum it well; put your Plums in a Pot; pour the Jelly on them ſcalding hot: When they are almoſt cold, heat them again; ſo do 'till they are tender, and then let them ſtand two or three Days, heating them every Day; then boil them 'till they look clear and jelly: Don't boil them too faſt.

To preserve White Pear-Plums.

SLIT your Plums, and ſcald them in a thin Syrup; as for drying them, put them in a thick Syrup of clarify'd Sugar, as much as will cover them; let them boil very ſlow, 'till they are very clear, ſometimes ſetting them off

off the Fire: They muſt have the Weight, or ſomething more, of clarify'd Sugar in the Syrup: When they are very tender and clear, put to a Pound of Plums (when they are raw) a Pint of Apple-Jelly, and a Pound of fine Sugar, and boil it 'till it jellies; before your Plums are cold put them into the Jelly, but not above half the Syrup they were boil'd in, and boil them together 'till they jelly well: Put them in Pots or Glaſſes, with Papers cloſe to them. You may keep ſome of them in Syrup, and put them in Jelly as you uſe them.

To make WHITE PEAR-PLUM CLEAR-CAKES.

TAKE a good Quantity of white Pear-Plums, as many as you think will make three Pints, with as much boiling Water as will cover them; boil them very faſt, 'till they are all to Pieces; then have ready three Pints of Apple-Jelly, and put it to the Plums, boiling them very faſt together; then

then run it thro' a Jelly-bag: To a Pint put a Pound and half of ſifted Sugar; firſt boil the Jelly, and ſhake in the Sugar; let it ſcald on the Fire 'till it is melted; put it in Pots in the Stove; dry and turn it as other Clear-Cakes.

To make WHITE PLUM-PASTE.

TAKE a Pound of fine Sugar, and a Pint of Water, or more, as the Quantity you intend to make requires; ſet it on the Fire, let it boil, and ſet a Pan of Water to boil; when it boils, put in your Plums; let them juſt boil, and then take them out with a Ladle, as they ſlip their Skins off; take off the Skins, and put the Plums into the Syrup; do this as faſt as you can, that they may not turn: Boil them all to Pieces; and to a Quart of Plums put a Pint of Apple-Jelly; boil them well together, and rub it thro' a Hair Sieve; to a Pint of this put a Pound and a half of ſifted Sugar; let the Jelly boil before you ſhake

ſhake the Sugar, and let it ſcald 'till the Sugar is well melted; ſkin it, put it in Pots, and dry it in the Stove.

To make Red Plum Clear-Cakes.

TAKE white Pear-Plums, half White and half Black, or if you have no Black, one third of Damſins, and as much Water as will cover them; boil them very well; and to a Quart of the Plums put a Quart of Apple-Jelly; boil them very well together; run it thro' a Jelly-bag; to a Pint of the Jelly put a Pound and Half of Sugar; let the Jelly boil, then ſhake in the Sugar; let it ſcald, but not boil; put it thro' a thin Strainer in a broad Pan, to take off the Scum, and put it in Pots in a Stove: When it is candy'd, turn it as other Clear-Cakes: You may make it paler or redder, as you beſt like, with more or leſs black Plums.

To make RED PLUM-PASTE.

TAKE half white and half red Plums, as you did for the Clear-Cakes; boil them with as much Water as will cover them; then, to a Quart of Plums put a Pint of Apple-Jelly; let them boil well together; rub it thro' an Hair Sieve; to a Pint of Jelly put in a Pound and half of Sugar; boil the Jelly, and ſhake in the Sugar; let it ſcald 'till the Sugar is melted, ſkin it well, and fill in Pots; dry it as other Cakes: You may put ſome of this in Plates, and make Fruit-Jambals.

To dry PLUMS *like the* FRENCH PLUMS, *with Stones in them.*

WHEN you have laid out all your Plums that are to be ſtopt, put white Pear-Plums, or any large black Plums, in an Earthen Pot, and make your Plum-Syrup almoſt ſcalding hot; put it to the Plums,

Plums, and ſcald the Syrup every Day, 'till the Plums are tender and red; then lay them on Sieves, and dry them in an Oven, turning them every Day 'till they are dry; then lay them between Papers, and keep them in a dry Place.

To dry PEACHES.

STONE the largeſt white *Newington* Peaches, and pare them, and have ready a Pan over the Fire with boiling Water; put in the Peaches, and let them boil 'till they are tender; then lay them on a Sieve to drain out all the Water; weigh them, and lay them in the Pan you boil them in, and cover them with their Weight in Sugar; let them lye two or three Hours; then boil them 'till they are clear, and the Syrup pretty thick; ſet them by cover'd, with a Paper cloſe to them; the next Day ſcald them very well, ſetting them off the Fire and on again, 'till the Peaches are thorough hot; repeat this for three Days; then lay them on

 Plates

Plates to dry, and turn them every Day 'till dry.

To make PEACH-CHIPS.

PARE the Peaches, and cut them in thin Chips; to four Pound of Chips put three Pound and a Half of fine beaten Sugar; let the Sugar and Chips lye a little while, 'till the Sugar is well melted, then boil them faſt 'till they are clear; about half an Hour will do them enough; ſet them by 'till the next Day, then ſcald them very well two Days, and lay them on earthen Plates in a Stove; ſift on them fine Sugar, through a Lawn Sieve; turn them every Day, ſifting them 'till almoſt dry; then lay them on a Sieve a Day or two more in the Stove: Lay them in a Box cloſe together, and when they have lain ſo a Week, pick them aſunder, that they may not be in Lumps.

To preserve or dry NUTMEG-PEACHES.

PEEL the Peaches, and put them in boiling Water; let them boil a Quarter of an Hour; lay them to drain, weigh them, and to a Pound of Peaches put a Pound of fine Sugar beaten very ſmall; when the Sugar is pretty well melted, boil them very faſt 'till they are clear; ſet them by 'till they are cold; then ſcald them very well; take to every Pint of Peach a Pint of Codling-Jelly and a Pound of Sugar; boil it 'till it jellies very well, then put in the Peaches and half the Syrup; let them boil faſt; then put them in Pots or Glaſſes: If you wou'd dry them, ſcald them three or four Days, and dry them out of their Syrup.

To preserve CUCUMBERS.

TAKE Cucumbers of the ſame Bigneſs that you wou'd to pickle; pick them freſh, green, and free from Spots; boil them in Water 'till they are

are tender; then run a Knitting-needle through them the long Way, and ſcrape off all Roughneſs; then green them, which is done thus: Let your Water be ready to boil, take it off, and put in a good Piece of Roach-Allum; ſet it on the Fire, and put in the Cucumbers; cover them cloſe 'till you ſee they look green; weigh them, and take their Weight in ſingle-refin'd Sugar clarify'd; to a Pound of Sugar put a Pint of Water; put your Cucumbers in; boil them a little cloſe-cover'd; ſet them by, and boil them a little every Day for four Days; then take them out of your Syrup, and make a Syrup of double-refin'd Sugar, a Pound of Sugar and half a Pint of Water to every Pound of Cucumbers; put in your Cucumbers, and boil them 'till they are clear; then put in the Juice of two or three Lemmons, and a little Orange-flower-water, and give them a Boil altogether: You may either lay them out to dry, or keep them in Syrup; but every Time you take any out, make the other ſcalding hot, and they will keep two or three Years.

To dry GREEN FIGS.

TAKE the white Figs at the full Bigneſs, before they turn Colour; ſlit them at the Bottom; put your Figs in ſcalding Water; keep them in a Scald, but not boil them 'till they are turn'd yellow; then let them ſtand 'till they are cold; they muſt be cloſe cover'd, and ſomething on them to keep them under Water; ſet them on the Fire again, and when they are ready to boil, put to them a little Verdigreaſe and Vinegar, and keep them in a Scald 'till they are green; then put them in boiling Water; let them boil 'till they are very tender; drain them well from the Water, and to every Pound clarify a Pound and Half of ſingle-refin'd Sugar, and when the Sugar is cold put in the Figs; let them lye all Night in the cold Syrup; the next Day boil them 'till they are very clear, and the Syrup thick, and ſcald them every Day for a Week; then lay them to dry in a Stove, turning them every Day; weigh your Figs when they are raw; and when you clarify your Sugar, put half

half a Pint of Water to a Pound of Sugar: If your Figs grow too dry, you may put them in their Syrup again; they will look new to the End of the Year.

To dry BLACK FIGS.

WEigh the Figs, and ſlit them at the Bottom; put them into boiling Water, and boil them 'till they are very tender; drain them well from the Water; then make a Syrup of clarify'd ſingle-refin'd Loaf-Sugar, with their Weight, and half a Pint of Water to a Pound of Sugar; when the Syrup is cold put in your Figs; let them lye all Night; the next Day boil them 'till they are very clear, and ſcald them every Day 'till the Syrup is very thick; then lay them out as you uſe them; but heat the Syrup after you have taken ſome out, or they will not keep: If they grow too dry, you may put them in the Syrup again, ſcalding the Syrup.

To preserve GRAPES.

PEEL the Grapes and ſtone them; put them in a Pan, cover them very cloſe; firſt let them boil, and ſet them ſometimes on and off the Fire, 'till they are very green; then drain all the Juice from them; and to a Pint of Grapes put a Pound and a Half of Sugar, and half a Pint of Apple-Jelly; let them boil very faſt 'till they are clear, and jelly very well: Put them in Pots or Glaſſes, with Paper cloſe to them.

To dry GRAPES.

TAKE the large Bell-Grapes, juſt before they are ripe; ſtone them in Bunches, and put them into ſcalding Water, covering them cloſe with Vine-Leaves, and a Cover on the Pan; keep them in a Scald, putting them on and off the Fire 'till they are green; then give them a Boil in the Water, drain them on a Sieve, and to every Pound of Grapes make a thick Syrup of a Pound and a Half of clarify'd Sugar; and when the Syrup is cold, put in the Grapes, and ſcald them every Day 'till the Syrup is thick, but never let them boil; then lay them out on Earthen Plates, and ſift them very well with Sugar; dry them in a Stove, and turn and ſift them every Day.

To dry BARBERRIES.

TAKE Barberries, ſtone them, and tye them in Bunches, or looſe in Sprigs, which you pleaſe; weigh them, and to every Pound of Barberries clarify two Pound of Sugar; make your Syrup with ſomething more than half a Pint of Water to a Pound of Sugar; put the Barberries into the Syrup when it is ſcalding hot; ſet it on the Fire, and let them juſt boil; then ſet them by, with a Paper cloſe to them; the next Day make them ſcalding hot, doing ſo for two Days; but be ſure they never boil after the firſt Time; when they are cold, lay them

out

out on Earthen Plates; sift them well with Sugar, and the next Day turn them on a Sieve; sift them again, and turn them every Day 'till they are dry: Your Stove must not be too hot.

To preserve BARBERRIES.

STONE the Barberries in Sprigs; and to a Pound of Barberries make a Syrup of a Pound and a Half of fine Sugar, with half a Pint of Water to a Pound of Sugar: Put the Barberries in the Syrup, and let them have a Boil; scald them every Day for four or five Days, but don't let them boil: Put them in a Pot, and when you use any, heat the rest, or they will not keep.

To make BARBERRY-DROPS.

TAKE a good Quantity of Barberries, strip them off the Stalks; put to them a little Water, to keep them

 from

from Burning; boil them, and maſh them as they boil, till they are very dry; then rub them through an Hair Sieve, and afterwards ſtrain them through a Strainer, that there may be none of the black Noſes in it; make it ſcalding hot, and to half a Pint of the Pulp put a Pound of the ſifted Sugar; let it ſcald, and drop it on Boards or Glaſſes; then put it in a Stove, and turn it when it is candy'd.

To make WHITE QUINCE-MARMALET.

PARE Quinces, and quarter them, putting as much Water as will cover them, and boil them all to Pieces to make Jelly; run it through a Jelly-bag; then take a Pound of Quince, pare, quarter, and cut out all the Hard of it; and to a Pound of Quinces put a Pound and a Half of Sugar fine beaten, and half a Pint of Water, and let it boil 'till it is very clear; keep it ſtirring, and it will

break

break as much as ſhou'd be; when the Sugar is boil'd to be very thick, almoſt a Candy, put in half a Pint of Jelly, and let it boil very faſt 'till it jellies: As ſoon as you take it off, put in the Juice of a Lemon; ſkim it well, and put it in Pots or Glaſſes: It is the better for having Lumps in it.

To make RED QUINCE-MARMALET.

PARE the Quinces, quarter them, and cut out all that is hard; to a Pound of Quinces put in a Pound and a H lf of Sugar, and h lf a Pint or Juice of Barberries, boil'd with Water, as you do Jelly, or other Fruit; boil it very faſt, and break it very ſmall; when it is all to Pieces, and jellies, it is enough: If you wou'd have the Marmalet of a very fine Colour, put a few black Bullace to the Barberries when you make the Jelly.

To preserve Whole Quinces.

TAKE a Pound of Quince par'd and quarter'd, cut out all the Hard, put to it a Pound of fine Sugar and half a Pint of Water, and let it boil very faſt 'till it is all to Pieces; take it off the Fire, and break it very well, that there be no Lumps in it; boil it 'till it is very thick and well jelly'd; then take fine Muſlin, and put your Quinces into it, and tye it up round. This Quantity will make three Quinces. Set them into three Pots, or *China* Cups, that will juſt hold one; cut off the Stalk-End of the Quince, and put it in the Pot or Cup, to make a Dent in the Quince, that it may be like a whole Quince; let them ſtand two or three Days, that they may be very ſtiff; take them out of the Muſlin, and make a ſtrong Jelly with Apples and Quinces: Take two Pints of Jelly and two Pound of Sugar, boil it faſt 't ll it jellies very well; then put in the Quinces, and let them have two or three Boils to make them hot; put them in in Pots or Glaſſes, with Paper cloſe to them.

To make QUINCE-CHIPS.

PARE the Quinces, and ſlice them into Water; put them into boiling Water; let them boil faſt 'till they are very tender, but not ſo ſoft as to break them: Take them out with a Skimmer, lay them on a Sieve 'till they are well drain'd, and have ready a very thick Syrup of clarify'd Sugar; put them into as much as will cover them, then boil them 'till they are very clear, and the next Day ſcald them; and if you ſee they want Syrup, put in a Pint more, but let it be very thick: Scald them twice more, then lay them out on Earthen Plates in a Stove, ſift them well with Sugar: Turn them and ſift them 'till they are dry.

To

To make QUINCE-PASTE.

PARE the Quinces, and quarter them; to a Pound of Quince put half a Pound of Sugar and half a Pint of Water; boil it faſt 'till the Quinces are all to Pieces; then rub it very fine, 'till there be no Lumps in it, and put to it a Pint of Jelly of Quince, boil'd with as much Water as will cover them, and run through a Jelly-bag; boil the Quinces Jelly together, and to a Pint of it put a Pound and a Quarter of fine Sugar; let it ſcald, but not boil, 'till the Sugar is melted; ſkim it, and put it in the Stove; turn it when it is candy'd; twice turning will do.

To make QUINCE CLEAR-CAKES.

PARE, quarter, and boil the Quince with as much Water as will cover it, putting in a little more as it boils, but not too much; let it be a very ſtrong Jelly, and run it through a Jelly-bag; put a Pound and a Half of the fineſt ſifted Sugar to a Pint of Jelly; let the Jelly boil, then put in the Sugar, and let it ſcald 'till the Sugar is melted; then put it through a Strainer, laid in a broad Earthen Pan; fill it in little Pots, and when it is hard candy'd, turn it on Glaſſes as other Clear-Cakes: Colour the Jelly, if you wou'd have any Red Quince Clear-Cakes, with the Jelly of black Bullace, and let it boil after the Red is in, before you put in the Sugar.

To preſerve Golden *or* Kentish-Pippins.

BOIL the Rind of an Orange very tender, and let it lye in Water two or three Days; then make a ſtrong Jelly with Pippins, and run it through a Jelly-bag. Take Golden-Pippins, pare them, and ſcoop out all the Coar at the Stalk End: To twelve

Pippins put two Pound of Sugar and three Quarters of a Pint of Water, boil the Sugar and ſkim it; put in the Pippins and the Orange-Rind cut into thin Slices; let them boil as faſt as they can 'till the Sugar is very thick, and almoſt a Candy; then put in a Pint of the Pippin-Jelly, and boil them very faſt 'till they jelly very well; then put in the Juice of a Lemmon, give it one Boil, and put them in Pots or Glaſſes, with the Orange mix'd with them. The *Kentiſh* Pippins are better in Quarters than whole.

To preſerve WHOLE ORANGES *or* LEMMONS.

RASP them very thin, juſt the Outſide Rind off; lay them in Water twenty four Hours; then ſet them on the Fire with a good Quantity of Water; let them boil 'till they are very tender; then put them in cold Water again, and let them lye two Days; the Lemmons need not lye but one Day; then, to four Oranges or Lemmons put two

two Pound of fine Sugar and a Pint of Water; boil and ſkim it, and when it is cold, put in the Oranges or Lemmons, and let them lye four or five Days in cold Syrup; then boil them 'till they are clear; ſet them by in an Earthen Pan a Day or two more; then boil them again, and put them in Jelly, thus: Take Pippin-Jelly, and to a Pint put a Pound of fine Sugar; boil it 'till the Jelly is very ſtrong; then heat your Oranges, and put them to the Jelly, with half their Syrup; boil them very faſt a Quarter of an Hour; when you take them off the Fire, put in the Juice of two or three Lemmons; put them in Pots that will hold the Jelly: To four Oranges you may put one Pint and a Half of Jelly, and one Pound and a Half of Sugar. Lemmons muſt be done by themſelves. *Sevil* Oranges and *Malaga* Lemmons are beſt.

To dry ORANGES *in* KNOTS, *or* LEMMONS.

RASP the Oranges or Lemmons with a ſharp Knife, as thin and as ſmall as you can, and break the Raſping as little as you can, that the Outſide Rind may make but two or three Knots; then cut the Oranges, and pick out all the Meat; and the white Rind makes another Sort of Knots: Let both the Rinds lye two Days in a Sieve, or broad Pan, before you boil them, or they will break; then put them in cold Water, and boil them about an Hour; let them drain well from the Water, and clarify as much ſingle-refin'd Sugar as will cover them very well; when the Syrup is cold put them in, and let them ſtand four or five Days; dry them out as you uſe them; and when you take any out to dry, boil them which you leave in the Syrup. They muſt be candy'd out thus: Take as many as you deſire to dry; the white Halves muſt be cut in Rings, or Quarters, as you like them; then take

take as much clarify'd Sugar as will cover them; boil them very faſt a great while, 'till the Sugar ſhall blow, which you may ſee, if you put in a Ladle with Holes, and blow thro', you will ſee the Sugar fly from the Ladle; then take it off, and rub the Candy againſt the Pan Sides, and round the Bottom, 'till the Sugar looks Oily; then put them out on a Sieve, to let the Sugar run from them; and as quick as poſſible lay them in Knots on another Sieve; ſet them in a Stove, they will be dry in an Hour or two: If you do but a few at a Time, the Syrup you put to them at firſt will do them out. Whole Oranges or Lemmons are done the ſame Way, only boil the whole after they are raſp'd, and cut a Hole at the Top, and pick out all the Meat after they are boil'd, and before they are put in the Syrup; and when they are laid on a Sieve to dry, put the Piece in again.

To make CHINA CHIPS.

CUT the Rind of *China* Oranges in long Chips, but very thin, and with none of the White; boil them in Water 'till they are very tender; then drain them, and put them into a very thick cold Syrup of clarify'd Sugar; let them lye a Day or two; then ſcald them, and when they are cold lay them to dry on Earthen Plates in a Stove. *Sevil* Oranges will do the ſame Way, if you like them with a little Sugar, and very bitter.

To make ORANGE-PASTE.

RASP the Oranges, and you may make the Outſide for Knots; then cut the Oranges, and pick out all the Meat, and all the Stones from the Meat; boil the white Rinds very tender, drain them well, and beat them fine; to a Pint and half of the Meat put a Pound of the beaten Rind; mix it well, make it ſcalding hot; then put in in three Pound of fine Sugar ſifted thro' an Hair Sieve; ſtir it well in, and ſcald it 'till the Sugar is well melted; then put in the Juice of three large Lemmons: Put the Paſte in flat Earthen Pans, or deep Plates; ſet it in the Stove 'till it is candy'd; then drop it on Glaſſes: Let what is too thin to drop ſtand 'till 'tis candy'd again: Once turning will dry it. *Sevil* Oranges make the beſt.

To make ORANGE-DROPS.

TAKE about a Dozen Oranges, ſqueeze out the Juice, boil the Rind very tender, cut out moſt of the White, and beat the yellow Rind very fine; rub it thro' an Hair Sieve, and to a Pound of the Pulp put a Pound and a Half of fine Sugar, ſifted thro' an Hair Sieve; mix it well in, and put in the Juice 'till you make it thin enough to drop from a Tea-Spoon: Drop it on Glaſſes, and ſet it by the Fire; let it ſtand there about two Hours, and then put it in a Stove; the

next

next Day turn it: it will be dry in twenty four Hours.

To make ORANGE-MARMALET.

RASP the Oranges, cut out the Meat, boil the Rinds very tender, and beat them very fine; then take three Pound of fine Sugar and a Pint of Water, boil and ſkim it; then put in a Pound of Rind, boil it faſt 'till the Sugar is very thick; then put in a Pint of the Meat of the Orange, (the Seeds being pick'd out) and a Pint of very ſtrong Pippin-Jelly; boil all together very faſt, 'till it jellies very well, which will be half an Hour; then put it in Pots or Glaſſes, with Papers cloſe to it.

To make ORANGE *or* LEMMON CLEAR-CAKES.

MAKE a very ſtrong Pippin-Jelly; when it is run thro' a Jelly-bag, take a Quart of Jelly, and the Meat

Meat of three or four Oranges, boil them together, and rub it thro' a Jelly-bag again; then take a Quarter of a Pint of Orange-Juice, a Quarter of a Pound of fine Sugar, and let it have a Boil; then put it into your Jelly, but first meaſure your Jelly; put half the Syrup of the Oranges to a Pint of Juice, and the Outſide of an Orange, boil'd in two or three Waters, and ſhred very fine; make them ſcalding hot together; then to a Pint of Jelly take a Pound and a Half of Sugar, boiling the Sugar to a Candy; then put in your Jelly, but not altogether; becauſe if it all boil in the hot Sugar, it will not dry: As ſoon as it has done boiling, put in the reſt; ſet it over the Fire 'till all the Candy is well melted; but take Care it does not boil; then fill it in little Pots, dry and turn it on Glaſſes, as other Clear-Cakes. Lemmons are done the ſame Way.

To make POMEGRANATE CLEAR-CAKES.

MAKE a ſtrong Pippin-Jelly, and ſlice a Lemmon into it, Rind and all; boil it well, and run it thro' the Jelly-bag again; then colour it as you like it: To a Pint of the Jelly take half a Quarter of Orange-Syrup, made as for Orange Clear-Cakes; let it have a Boil together, and boil a Pound and a Half of Sugar to a Candy; put your Jelly to the Candy, a little at a Time, 'till the Sugar has done boiling, then put in all the reſt; ſcald it 'till the Candy is well melted, fill it in Pots, and dry it as other Clear-Cakes.

The Colour is made thus: Take as much Carmine as you can have for Half-a-Crown, put to it two Ounces of Sugar, and as much Water as will wet it; give it a Boil, and then colour your Jelly with it.

To make ORANGE-HALVES, *or* QUARTERS, *with the Meat in them.*

RASP the Oranges round and thin, cut them in Halves, pick out the Meat, boil the Halves very tender, then take half of them, that are cleareſt and beſt, and put them in a thick cold Syrup, as much as will cover them; the Syrup muſt be made with fine Sugar, half a Pint of Water to a Pound of Sugar; beat the other Half of the Rinds very fine; pick the Seeds out of the Meat; and to a Pint of the Meat put half a Pound of the beaten Rinds; ſcald it very well, and ſtir it into a Pound and a Half of ſifted Sugar; ſcald it 'till the Sugar is well melted; put in the Juice of a Lemmon or two; ſet it in a broad Earthen Pan in a Stove; when the Half Orange-Rinds have lain three or four Days in the Syrup, boil them very faſt 'till they are clear, and the Syrup very thick; when they are cold, lay them out on Earthen Plates in a Stove; the next Day, if you think they have not Sugar enough on them, dip them in the Syrup that runs from them; they muſt not have dry Sugar on them, but only a Gloſs; before they are quite dry, fill them with the Meat; ſet them on a Sieve, to dry in a Stove, which will be in a Day or two.

To preſerve CITRONS.

TAKE the largeſt *Malaga* Citrons, cut them in four Quarters, ſcrape the Rind a little, but not all the Yellow off; cut out all the Meat; lay them in Water all Night; then boil them very tender, and lay them in Water another Night; then drain them very well, and to three Pound of Citron take four Pound of fine Sugar and two Quarts of Water; make the Sugar and Water juſt warm, put in the Citron, boil it half an Hour, and ſet it by 'till the next Day; then boil it 'till it is very clear, and put in a Pound more of Sugar, juſt wet with Water, boiling it faſt 'till it is melted:

Put in the Juice of four Lemmons, and put it up in large Pots.

To make CITRON MARMALET.

BOIL the Citron very tender, cut off all the yellow Rind, beat the White very well in a Tray, or wooden Bowl, ſhred the Rind, and to a Pound of the Pulp and Rind take a Pound and a Half of Sugar and half a Pint of Water; when it boils, put in the Citron, boil it very faſt 'till it is clear; then put in half a Pint of Pippin-Jelly, and boil it 'till it jellies very well; then put in the Juice of a Lemmon: Put it in Pots or Glaſſes.

To candy ORANGE-FLOWERS.

TAKE the Flowers full blown, pick the white Leaves, and put them in Water an Hour or two; then put them into boiling Water, letting them boil 'till they are tender; then drain them

them from that Water, and let them lye in cold Water, 'till you make a Syrup of very fine Sugar, as much as you think will cover them; to a Pound of Sugar put three Quarters of a Pint of Water; and when the Syrup is cold, put in the Leaves, and let them lye all Night; ſcald them the next Day, and let them lye in the Syrup two or three Days; then make a Syrup, (if you have a Pound of the Flowers) with a Pound and Half of fine Sugar and half a Pint of Water; boil and ſkim it, and when it is cold, drain the Flowers from the thin Syrup, and put them in the Thick; let them lye two or three Days; then make them juſt hot, and in a Day or two more lay them out on Glaſſes: Spread them very thin, ſift them with fine Sugar, and put them in a Stove: Four or five Hours will dry them on one Side; then ſcrape them on Paper with the wet Side uppermoſt, and ſet them in the Stove 'till they are almoſt dry; then pick them aſunder, and let them be in a Stove 'till they are quite dry: You may put ſome of them in Jelly, if you like it.

To make ROCK-SUGAR.

TAKE a red Earthen Pot, that will hold about four Quarts, (thoſe Pots that are ſomething leſs at the Top and Bottom than in the Middle) ſtick it pretty thick with the Sticks of a white Wiſk, a-croſs, one over the other; ſet it before a good Fire, that it may be very hot againſt your Sugar is boil'd; then take ten Pound of double-refin'd Sugar finely beaten, the Whites of two Eggs beaten to a Froth in half a Pint of Water, and mix it with the Sugar; then put to it a Quart of Orange-flower-water and three half Pints of Water, ſetting it on a quick Fire; when it boils thoroughly put in half a Pint of Water more to raiſe the Scum, and let it boil up again; then take it off and ſkim it; do ſo two or three Times, 'till it is very clear; then let it boil, 'till you find it draw between your Fingers, which you muſt often try, with taking a little in the Ladle; and as it cools, it will draw like a Thread; then put it into the hot Pot, covering it cloſe, and

ſet-

ſetting it in a very hot Stove for three Days: It muſt ſtand three Weeks; but after the three firſt Days a moderate Fire will do; but never ſtir the Pots, nor let the Stove be quite cold: Then take it out, and pour out all the Syrup, the Rock will be on the Sticks and the Pot-ſides: ſet the Pots in cold Water, in a Pan, on the Fire, and when it is thorough hot all the Rock will ſlip out, and fall moſt of it in ſmall Pieces; the Sticks you muſt juſt dip in hot Water, and that will make the Rock ſlip off; then put in a good Handful of dry Orange-Flowers, and take a Ladle with Holes, and put the Rock and Flowers in it, as much as will make as big a Lump as you wou'd like; dip it in ſcalding Water, and lay it on a Tin Plate; then make it up in handſome Lumps, and as hollow as you can: When it is ſo far prepar'd, put it in a hot Stove, and the next Day it will ſtick together; then take it off the Plates, and let it lye two or three Hours in the Stove; if there be any large Pieces, you may make Bottoms of them, and lay ſmall Pieces on them.

To make FRUIT-BISCUIT.

SCALD the Fruit, dry it well from the Water, and rub it through a Hair Sieve; ſtir it in a Pan over a ſlow Fire, 'till it is pretty dry; the ſtiffer it is, the better; then take two Pound of fine Sugar, ſifted thro' an Hair Sieve, and a Spoonful of Gum-Dragon ſteep'd very well, and ſtrain'd, and about a Quarter of a Pound of Fruit; mix it well with Sugar, beat it with a Biſcuit-Beater, and take the Whites of twelve Eggs, beat up to a very ſtiff Froth; put in but a little at a Time, beating it 'till it is all in, and looks as white as Snow, and very thick; then drop it on Papers, and put it in an Oven; the Oven muſt be very cool, and ſhut up, to make them riſe: The Lemmon-Biſcuit is made the ſame Way, only inſtead of Fruit put in the Juice of three Lemmons; leſs will make two Pound; it muſt have Juice enough to make it to a Paſte, and the Rinds of two Lemmons gra-ed; and when it is beaten enough, put in a little Muſk, or Amber, and drop and bake it as other.

To make all Sorts of SUGAR-PASTE.

SIFT your Sugar thro' a Lawn Sieve, then ſift ſome Starch as fine; to a Pound of Sugar put a Quarter of a Pound of Starch; make it of what Colour you pleaſe, into a ſtiff Paſte; putting thereto Gum-Dragon well ſteep'd in Orange-Flower-Water; beat it well in a Mortar, and make it in Knots or Shells in a Mould or Moſs, with rubbing it thro' an Hair Sieve: The Red muſt be colour'd with Carmine; the Yellow with Gumboodge, ſteep'd in Water, and put to the Gum; the Green is made with Yellow Gum, putting to it Stone-Blue ſteep'd in Water; the Brown with Chocolate, and the Blue with Smalt.

To make CHOCOLATE-ALMONDS.

TAKE two Pound of fine ſifted Sugar, half a Pound of Chocolate grated, and ſifted thro' an Hair Sieve, a Grain of Muſk, a Grain of Amber, and two Spoonfuls of Ben; make this up to a ſtiff Paſte with Gum-Dragon ſteep'd well in Orange-Flower-Water; beat it well in a Mortar; make it in a Mould like Almonds; lay them to dry on Papers, but not in a Stove.

To make WORMWOOD-CAKES.

SIFT fine Sugar thro' an Hair Sieve, and cover it with Carmine; wet it more than a Candy with Water; boil it pretty faſt 'till it is almoſt at a Candy Height; then put in about three Drops of Spirit of Wormwood, and fill it into little Coffins made of Cards; when it boils in the Coffins it is enough; you muſt not boil above half a Pound at a Time, or leſs: The spirit of Wormwood muſt be that which looks black, and as thick as Oil, and muſt have two or three Boils in the Cakes after you put it in.

To make HONYCOMB-CAKES *of* ORANGE-FLOWER-VIOLET *of* COWSLIPS.

TAKE about half a Pound of fine Sugar, ſifted thro' an Hair Sieve, wet it more than for a Candy, with Orange-Flower-Water, for the Orange-Flower-Cakes, and fair Water for the other Cakes; boil it almoſt to Candy Height, and then put in the Leaves of the Flowers; boil them a little in the Candy, or it will be too thin; then put it in Card-Coffins.

To make ICE ALMOND-CAKES.

BEAT a Pound of Almonds very fine, with Roſe-Water, to keep them from Oiling; mix them with half

a

a Pound of ſifted Sugar, make them up into little long or round Cakes, which you like beſt; put them in a Stove or before a Fire, 'till they are dry on one Side, and then turn them; and when they are dry on both Sides, take very fine Sugar ſifted; to a Pound take as much White of Eggs as will juſt wet it; beat it with a Spoon, and as it grows white put in a little more Egg, 'till it is thin enough to ice the Cakes; then ice firſt one Side, and when that is dry before the Fire, ice the other: Be ſure one Side is dry before you do the other.

To make BEAN'D-BREAD.

BLANCH half a Pound of Almonds, ſlice them thin the long Way, lay them in Roſe-Water all Night; then drain them from the Water, and ſet them by the Fire, ſtirring them 'till they are a little dry and very hot; then put to them fine Sugar ſifted, enough to hang about them. (They muſt not be ſo wet as to make the Sugar

gar like Paſte; nor ſo dry, but that the Sugar may hang together.) Then lay them in Lumps on Wafer-Paper, and ſet them on Papers in an Oven, after Puffs, or any very cool Oven that Pies have been baked in.

To make ORANGE *or* LEMMON-PUFFS.

TAKE a Pound of fine ſifted Sugar, and grate the Outſide Rind of two large Oranges or Lemmons; put the Rind to the Sugar, and beat them well together in a Mortar; grind it well with a Peſtle, and make it up to a ſtiff Paſte with Gum-Dragon well ſteep'd; then beat the Paſte again, rowl or ſquare it, and bake it in a cool Oven, on Papers and Tin-Plates.

To make ALMOND-PASTE, *either* BITTER *or* SWEET: *The* BITTER *are* RATAFEA.

BLANCH and beat a Pound of Almonds; put in juſt Roſe-Water enough to keep them from Oiling; then take a Pound of fine Sugar, and boil it to a Candy; and when it is almoſt at a Candy Height, put in the Almonds; ſtir them over a cool Fire 'till it is a very dry ſtiff Paſte, and almoſt cold, and ſet it by 'till it is quite cold; then beat it well in a Mortar, and put to it a Pound and a Half of fine ſifted Sugar; rub it very well together, and make it up with a Spoonful of well-ſteep'd Gum-Dragon and Whites of Eggs, whip'd to a Froth; then ſquirt it, and bake it in a cool Oven; put into the Sweet-Almonds the Rind of a Lemmon grated, but none in the Bitter: If you don't make the firſt Paſte ſtiff, they will run about the Oven. Bake them on Papers and Tin-Plates.

To make Little Round Ratafea-Puffs.

TAKE half a Pound of Kernels, or Bitter-Almonds, beat very ſtiff, and a Pound and a Half of ſifted Sugar; make it up to a ſtiff Paſte with White of Eggs whip'd to a Froth; beat it well in a Mortar, and make it up in little Loaves; then bake them in a very cool Oven, on Paper and Tin-Plates.

To make Brown-Wafers.

TAKE half a Pint of Milk and half a Pint of Cream, and put to it half a Pound of brown Sugar; melt and ſtrain it thro' a Sieve; take as much fine Flower as will make one half of the Milk and Cream very ſtiff, then put in the other Half; ſtir it all the while, that it may not be in Lumps; then put in two Eggs well beaten, a little Sack, ſome Mace ſhred fine,

fine, two or three Cloves beaten: Bake in Irons.

To make ALMOND-LOAVES.

BEAT a Pound of Almonds very fine, mix them well with three Quarters of a Pound of ſifted Sugar, ſet them over the Fire, keep them ſtirring 'till they are ſtiff, and put in the Rind of a Lemmon grated; make them up in little Loaves, ſhake them very well in the Whites of Eggs beat to a very ſtiff Froth, that the Egg may hang about them; then put them in a Pan with about a Pound of fine ſifted Sugar, ſhake them 'till they are well cover'd with the Sugar; divide them if they ſtick together, and add more Sugar, 'till they begin to be ſmooth, and dry; and when you put them on Papers to bake, ſhake them in a Pan that is juſt wet with White of Eggs, to make them have a Gloſs: Bake them after Biſcuit, on Papers and Tin-Plates.

To make CHOCOLATE-PUFFS.

TAKE a Pound of fine ſifted Sugar, and three Ounces of Chocolate grated, and ſifted thro' an Hair Sieve; make it up to a Paſte with White of Eggs whip'd to a Froth; then beat it well in a Mortar, and make it up in Loaves, or any Faſhion you pleaſe. Bake it in a cool Oven, on Papers and Tin-Plates.

To make RATAFEA-DROPS, *either of* APRICOCK-KERNELS, *or half* BITTER, *and half* SWEET-ALMONDS.

TAKE a Pound of Kernels or Almonds beat very fine with Roſe-Water; take a Pound of ſifted Sugar and the Whites of five Eggs beat to a Froth, mix them well together, and ſet them on a ſlow Fire; keep them ſtirring, 'till they begin to be ſtiff; when they are quite cold, make them in little round Drops; Bake them after the

the long Biſcuit, on Paper and Tin-Plates.

To make all Sorts of SUGAR-PUFFS.

TAKE very fine beaten Sugar, ſifted thro' a Lawn Sieve, make it up into a Paſte, with Gum-Dragon very well ſteep'd in Roſe-Water, or Orange-Flower-Water; beat it in a Mortar, ſquirt it, and bake it in a cool Oven. Colour the Red with Carmine, Blue with Powder-Blue, Yellow with ſteep'd Gamboodge put into Gum, and Yellow and Blue will make Green: Bake them after all other Puffs. Sugar the Papers well before you ſquirt the Puffs on Papers and Tin-Plates.

To make ALMOND-PASTE.

LAY a Pound of Almonds all Night in Water, and warm ſome Water the next Day to make them blanch, and then beat them very fine with Rose-Water; and to a Pound of Almonds take a Pound and a Quarter of fine Sugar; wet it with Water, boil it to a Candy Height, and then put to your Almonds three Spoonfuls of Rose-Water, mix it, and put it to the Candy; set it over the Fire 'till it is scalding hot, then put in the Juice of a Lemmon and the Rind grated; stir it over the Fire, and then drop it on Glass or clean Boards: Put it in a hot Stove; twelve Hours will dry it; then turn it, and dry it the other Side.

To make LONG-BISCUIT.

TAKE thirty Eggs, (the Whites of fourteen (break twenty eight of them; beat them very well with two Spoonfuls of Rose-Water; then put in three Pound of sifted Sugar, and beat it all the while the Oven is heating; then dry two Pound and a Quarter of fine Flower, let it be cold before you put it in, and put in the two

Eggs

Eggs left out; ſtir it well, and drop it. It muſt have a very quick Oven. Bake it almoſt as faſt as you can fill your Oven; the Papers muſt be laid on Tin-Plates, or they will burn at the Bottom. This ſame Biſcuit was the Queen's Seed-Biſcuit. Put to half this Quantity half a Pound of Caraway-Seeds, and bake it in large ſquare Tin-Pans, buttering the Pans: It bakes beſt in a cool Oven, after the Drop-Biſcuit is baked.

To make SPUNGE-BISCUIT.

TAKE the Yolks of eighteen Eggs, beat them well, the Whites of nine whip'd to a Froth, and beat them well together; put to them two Pound and two Ounces of ſifted Sugar, and have ready half a Pint of Water, with three Spoonfuls of Roſe-Water, boiling hot; and as you beat the Eggs and Sugar, put in the hot Water, a little at a Time; then ſet the Biſcuit over the Fire, (it muſt be beat in a Braſs or Silver Pan) keeping it beating, 'till it is

ſo

ſo hot that you can't hold your Finger in it; then take it off, and beat it 'till 'tis almoſt cold; then put in a Pound and Half of Flower well dry'd, and the Rind of two Lemmons grated. Bake it in little long Pans butter'd, and in a quick Oven: Sift Sugar over them before you put them in the Oven.

To make round BISCUIT *with* CORIANDER SEEDS.

TAKE nine Eggs, and but four of the Whites, beat them very well, put to them eight Spoonfuls of Roſe-Water, and eight of Orange-Flower-Water; beat the Eggs and Water a Quarter of an Hour; then put in a Pound of ſifted Sugar, three Quarter of a Pound of fine Flower well dry'd, beat this altogether an Hour and Half; then put in two Ounces of Coriander-Seeds a little bruis'd: When the Oven is ready, put them in little round Tin-Pans butter'd, and ſift Sugar over them. A cool Oven will bake them.

To

To make HARTSHORN-JELLY.

TAKE half a Pound of Hartſhorn, boil it in a Pipkin, with ſix Quarts of Spring-Water, 'till conſum'd to three Pints; let it ſtand all Night; then put to it half a Pound of fine Sugar, ſome Cinamon, Mace, and a Clove or two, and let it boil again; then put in the Whites of eight Eggs well beaten, letting it boil up again; then put in the Juice of four or five Lemmons, and half a Pint of *Rheniſh* Wine; let it juſt boil up, and then run it thro' a Jelly-bag 'till it is clear.

To make LEMMON-JELLY.

TAKE four Lemmons, raſp the Rinds into a Pint and half of Spring-Water, let it lye an Hour; and then put to it the Whites of five Eggs well beaten, half a Pound of Sugar, and the Juice of four Lemmons; when the Sugar is melted, ſtrain it thro' a thin Sieve or Strainer; then

take

take a little Powder of Turmerick, ty'd up in a Piece of Muslin, and lay it in a Spoonful of Water 'till it is wet; then squeeze a little into the Jelly, to make it Lemmon-Colour, but not too Yellow: Set it over the Fire, skim it, and when you see it jelly, put it in Glasses; if it boil, it will not be amiss.

To make BUTTER'D ORANGE.

RASP the Peel of two Oranges into half a Pint of Water; put to it half a Pint of Orange-Juice, and six Eggs, (but two of the Whites) and as much Sugar as will sweeten it; strain it, set it on the Fire, and when it is thick, put in a Piece of Butter as big as a Nut, keeping it stirring 'till it is cold.

To make ERINGO-CREAM.

TAKE a Quartern of Eringo's, cut them small, and boil them in half a Pint of Milk, 'till they are tender; then

then put to them a Pint of Cream and two Eggs, well beaten; ſet it on the Fire, and let it juſt boil; if you don't think it ſweet enough, put in a little Sugar.

To make BARLEY-CREAM.

TAKE two Ounces of Pearl-Barley, boil it in four or five Waters 'till it is very tender; then rub it thro' an Hair Sieve, and put it to a Pint of Cream, with an Egg well beaten; ſweeten it, and let it boil: If you pleaſe, you may leave ſome of the Barley whole in it.

To make RATAFEA-CREAM.

TAKE Kernels of Apricocks, beat them very fine, and to two Ounces put a Pint of Cream and two Eggs; ſweeten it, ſet it on the Fire, and let it boil 'till 'tis pretty thick: You may ſlice ſome of the Kernels thin, and put them in, beſides what is beaten.

To make ALMOND-BUTTER.

TAKE half a Pound of Almonds finely beaten, mix them in a Quart of Cream; ſtrain the Cream, and get out as much of the Almonds as you can thro' the Strainer; ſet it on the Fire, and when it is ready to boil, put in twelve Eggs (but three of the Whites) well beaten; ſtir it on the Fire 'till it turns to a Curd; then put in half a Pint of cold Milk, ſtir it well, and whey it in a Strainer: When 'tis cold ſweeten it.

To make a TRIFLE.

TAKE a Pint of Cream, and boil it, and when it is almoſt cold, ſweeten it, and put it in the Baſon you uſe it in; and put to it a Spoonful of Runnet; let it ſtand 'till it comes like

like Cheeſe: You may perfume it, or put in Orange-Flower-Water.

To make all Sorts of FRUIT-CREAM.

TAKE your Fruit, (ſcalded) or Sweet-meats, and rub it thro' an Hair Sieve, and boil your Cream; and when 'tis cold, put in your Fruit, 'till 'tis pretty thick.

To make SACK-POSSET, *or* SACK-CREAM.

TAKE twelve Eggs, (the Whites of but ſix) beat them, and put to them a Pint of Sack and half a Pound of Sugar; ſet them on a Fire, keeping them ſtirring 'till they turn white, and juſt begin to thicken; at the ſame Time on another Fire have a Quart of Cream, boil and pour it into the Eggs and Sack, give it a Stir round, and cover it a Quarter of an Hour before you eat it: The Eggs and Sack muſt be heated in the Baſon you uſe it in, and the Cream muſt boil before you ſet on the Eggs.

To make BLAMANGE.

TAKE two Ounces of Iſing-glaſs, ſteep it all Night in Roſe-Water; then take it out of the Water and put to it a Quart of Milk, and about ſix Laurel Leaves, breaking the Leaves into two or three Pieces; boil this 'till all the Iſing-glaſs is diſſolv'd, and the Milk diminiſh'd to leſs than a Pint; then put to it a Quart of Cream, letting it boil about half an Hour; then ſtrain it thro' a thin Strainer, leaving as little of the Iſing-glaſs in the Strainer as you can; ſweeten it, and, if you like it, put in a little Orange-Flower-Water; put it in a broad Earthen Pan, or *China* Diſh; the next Day, when you uſe it, cut it with a Jagging-Iron in long Slips, and lay it in Knots on the Diſh or Plate you ſerve it up in.

LEMMON-CREAM *made with* CREAM.

TAKE a Pint of Cream, the Yolks of two Eggs, and about a Quarter of a Pound of Sugar, boil'd with the Rind of a Lemmon cut very thin; when it is almoſt cold, take out the Rind, and put in the Juice of a large Lemmon, by Degrees, or it will turn, keeping it ſtirring 'till it is quite cold.

To make CITRON-CREAM.

TAKE half a Pound of Green Citron, cut it as thin as poſſible, and in ſmall long Pieces, but no longer than half an Inch: Put it in a Pint of Cream, with a Piece of the Rind of a Lemmon, and boil it a Quarter of an Hour; then ſweeten it, put in an Egg well beaten, and ſet it on the Fire again, 'till it grows thick; then put in the Juice of half a Lemmon, and ſtir it 'till 'tis cold.

To make PISTATO-CREAM.

TAKE half a Pound of Piſtato-Nuts, break them, and blanch the Kernels, and beat all (except a Dozen, that you muſt keep to ſlice, to lay on the Top of the Cream) with a little Milk; then put them into a Pint of Cream, with the Yolks of two Eggs, and ſweeten it with fine Sugar: To this Quantity put a Spoonful of the Juice of Spinage, ſtamp'd and ſtrain'd; ſet it all over the Fire, and let it juſt boil; and when you ſend it up, put the ſlic'd Kernels on the Top. If you like it thick, you may put in the White of one Egg.

To make CLOUTED-CREAM.

TAKE four Gallons of Milk, let it juſt boil up; then put in two Quarts of Cream, and when it begins to boil again, put it in two large Pans or Trays, letting it ſtand three Days; then take it from the Milk with a Skimmer

Skimmer full of Holes, and lay it in the Diſh you ſend it up in: Lay it high in the Middle, and a large handſome Piece on the Top, to cover all the reſt.

To make a very thick, raw CREAM.

TAKE two Trays, keep them boiling hot; and, when you bring your Milk, put it in the ſcalding-hot Tray, and cover it with the other hot Tray; and the next Day you will find a very thick Cream. This muſt be done the Night before you uſe it.

To make SPANISH-BUTTER.

TAKE two Gallons of Milk, boil it, and, whilſt boiling, put in a Quart of Cream; let it boil after the Cream is in; ſet it in two broad Pans or Trays, and let it ſtand two or three Days; then take the Cream from the Milk into a Silver Pan or wooden Bowl; put to it a Spoonful of Orange-Flower-Water,

Water, with a perfum'd Paſtel or two melted in it; and ſweeten it a little with ſifted Sugar: Then beat it with a Siiver Ladle or a wooden Beater, 'till it is ſtiff enough to lye as high as you wou'd have it: Be ſure to beat it all one Way, and not change your Hand.

To make ORANGE-BUTTER.

TAKE the Rind of two or three Oranges, and boil them very tender; then beat them very fine in a Mortar, and rub them thro' an Hair Sieve; then take a Quart of Cream, boil it, and put in the Yolks of ten Eggs, and the Whites of two; beat the Eggs very well before you put them to the boiling Cream; ſtir it all one Way, 'till it is a Curd; then whey it in a Strainer; when it is cold, mix in as much of the Orange as you think will make it taſte as you wou'd have it; then ſweeten it as you like it.

To make ALMOND-BUTTER.

TAKE a Pint of Milk, and about twelve large Laurel Leaves, break the Leaves in three or four Pieces; boil them in the Milk 'till it is half wasted; then put in a Quart of Cream, boil it with the Leaves and Milk; then strain it, and set it on the Fire again; when it boils, put in the Yolks of twelve Eggs, and the Whites of three, beating the Eggs very well; stir this 'till it is a Curd; put in about Half a Pint of Milk, let it have a Boil, then whey it in a Strainer. When it is cold, sweeten it. This tastes as well as that which has Almonds in it.

To make TROUT-CREAM.

HAVE three or four long Baskets made like a Fish; then take a Quart of new Milk and a Pint of Cream, sweeten it, and put in a little Orange-Flower-Water; make it as warm as Milk from the Cow; put in a Spoonful of Runnet, ſtir it, and cover it cloſe; and when it comes like a Cheeſe, wet the Baſkets, and ſet them hollow; lay the Cheeſe into them without breaking the Curd; as it wheys and ſinks, fill them up 'till all is in. When you ſend it up, turn the Baſkets on the Plates, and give it a Knock with your Hand, they will come out like a Fiſh: Whip Cream and lay about them. They will look well in any little Baſket that is ſhallow, if you have no long ones.

To make ALMOND-CREAM.

TAKE a Quarter of a Pound of Almonds, blanch and beat them very fine, put them to a Pint of Cream, boil the Almonds and Cream, then ſweeten it, and put it in the Whites of two Eggs well-beaten; ſet in on the Fire till it juſt boils and grow thick.

To make RAW-ALMOND, *or* RATAFEA-CREAM.

TAKE a Quarter of a Pound of bitter or ſweet Almonds, which you like beſt, blanch and beat them very fine, mix them with a Quart of Cream and the Juice of three or four Lemmons; ſweeten it as you like it, and whip it in a Tray with a Whiſk; as the Froth riſes, put it in a Hair Sieve to grow ſtiff; then fill your Baſon or Glaſſes.

To make CHOCOLATE-CREAM.

TAKE a Quarter of a Pound of Chocolate, breaking it into a Quarter of a Pint of boiling Water; mill it and boil it, 'till all the Chocolate is diſſolv'd; then put to it a Pint of Cream and two Eggs well-beaten; let it boil, milling it all the while; when it is cold, mill it again, that it may go up with a Froth.

To make SEGO-CREAM.

TAKE two Spoonfuls of Sego, boil it in two Waters, ſtraining the Water from it; then put to it half a Pint of Milk, boil it 'till 'tis very tender, and the Milk waſted; then put to it a Pint of Cream, a Blade of Mace, a little Piece of Lemmon-Peel, and two Eggs, (the White of but one) ſweeten and boil it 'till it is thick.

To ice CREAM.

TAKE Tin Ice-Pots, fill them with any Sort of Cream you like, either plain or ſweeten'd, or Fruit in it; ſhut your Pots very cloſe; to ſix Pots you muſt allow eighteen or twenty Pound of Ice, breaking the Ice very ſmall; there will be ſome great Pieces, which lay at the Bottom and Top: You muſt have a Pail, and lay ſome Straw at the Bottom; then lay in your Ice, and put in amongſt it a Pound of Bay-Salt; ſet in your Pots of Cream, and lay

lay Ice and Salt between every Pot, that they may not touch; but the Ice muſt lie round them on every Side; lay a good deal of Ice on the Top, cover the Pail with Straw, ſet it in a Cellar where no Sun or Light comes, it will be froze in four Hours, but it may ſtand longer; than take it out juſt as you uſe it; hold it in your Hand and it will ſlip out. When you wou'd freeze any Sort of Fruit, either Cherries, Raſberries, Currants, or Strawberries, fill your Tin-Pots with the Fruit, but as hollow as you can; put to them Lemmonade, made with Spring-Water and Lemmon-Juice ſweeten'd; put enough in the Pots to make the Fruit hang together, and put them in Ice as you do Cream.

To make HARTSHORN-FLUMMERY.

TAKE half a Pound of Hartſhorn, boil it in four Quarts of Water till it comes to one, or leſs; let it ſtand all Night; then beat and blanch a Quarter of a Pound of Almonds,

monds, melt the Jelly, mix the Almonds with it, and ſtrain it thro' a thin Strainer or Hair Sieve; then put in a Quarter of a Pint of Cream, a little Cinamon, and a Blade of Mace, boil theſe together, and ſweeten it: Put it into *China* Cups; when you uſe it, turn it out of the Cups, and eat it with Cream.

To make perfum'd PASTELS.

TAKE a Pound of Sugar ſifted thro' a Lawn Sieve, two Grains of Amber-Greaſe, one Grain of Muſk; grind the Amber and Muſk very fine, mix it with the Sugar, make it up to a Paſte with Gum-Dragon well ſteep'd in Orange-Flower-Water, and put in a Spoonful of Ben; beat the Paſte well in a Mortar, then roll it pretty thin, cut the Paſtels with a ſmall Thimble, and print them with a Seal; let them lye on Papers to dry; when they are dry, put them in a Glaſs that has a Cover, or in ſome cloſe Place, where they may not loſe their Scent.

To

To burn ALMONDS.

TAKE a Pound of *Jordan*-Almonds, ſet them before a hot Fire, or in an Oven, 'till they are very criſp; then take three Quarters of a Pound of Sugar, one Ounce of Chocolate grated, and a Quarter of a Pint of Water, and boil theſe almoſt to a Candy; then put in the Almonds, and let them be juſt hot; take them off and ſtir them, 'till the Sugar grows dry, and hangs about the Almonds: Put them out of the Pan on a Paper, and put them aſunder.

To make LEMMON-WAFERS.

TAKE fine ſifted Sugar, and put it in Spoons, colouring it in every Spoon of ſeveral Colours; wet it with Juice of Lemmon; this is to paint the Waters. Cut little ſquare Papers, of very thick but very fine Paper, (a Sheet will make two Dozen) then

then take a Spoonful of Sugar, wet it with Juice of Lemmon, let it be pretty ſtiff, hold the Spoon over the Fire 'till it grows thin, and is juſt ſcalding hot; then put a Tea-Spoonful on the Paper, rubbing it equally all over the Paper very thin; then paint it of what Colour you pleaſe, firſt ſcalding the Colours: When you ſee it grows dry, pin it at two Corners of the Paper; when they are cold, and you have made all you deſign to make, put them into a Box, and ſet them a Day or two by the Fire; then wet the Papers, with your Fingers dipt into Water, on the Outſide; let them lye a little, and the Papers will come off. The Colours are made thus: The Red with Carmine, the Blue with Smalt, the Green with Powder, call'd Green-Earth, and the Yellow with Saffron ſteep'd in Lemmon-Juice.

To candy little GREEN-ORANGES.

LAY the Oranges in Water three Days, ſhifting them every Day; then put them into ſcalding Water, keeping them in a Scald, cloſe cover'd, 'till they are green; then boil them 'till they are tender, and put them in Water for three Days more, ſhifting the Water every Day: Make a Syrup with their Weight in Sugar, Half a Pint of Water to a Pound of Sugar; when the Syrup is cold put the Oranges into it; let them lye two or three Days, and then candy them out as other Oranges.

To candy COWSLIPS, *or any* FLOWERS *or* GREENS *in Bunches.*

STEEP Gum-Arabick in Water, wet the Flowers with it, and ſhake them in a Cloth, that they may be dry; then dip them in fine ſifted Sugar, and hang them on a String, ty'd croſs a Chimney that has a Fire in it:

They muſt hang two or three Days 'till the Flowers are quite dry.

To make CARAMEL.

TAKE *China* Oranges, peel and ſplit them intoQuarters,but don't break the Skin; lay the Quarters before a Fire, turning them 'till the Skin is very dry; then take Half a Pound of Sugar ſifted thro' an Hair Sieve, put it in a Braſs or Silver Pan, and ſet it over a very ſlow Fire, keeping it ſtirring 'till all is melted, and looks pretty clear; then take it off the Fire, and put in your Orange-Quarters, one at a Time; take them out again as faſt as you can with a little Spoon, and lay them on a Diſh, that ſhou'd be butter'd, or they will not come off: The Sugar will keep hot enough to do any Plate full. You may do roaſted Cheſſnuts, or any Fruit in the Summer, firſt laying the Fruit before a Fire, or in a Stove, to make the Skin tough; for if any Wet come out, the Sugar will not ſtick to it: It muſt be done juſt when you uſe it, for it will not keep.

To make a good GREEN.

LAY an Ounce of Gumboodge in Water 'till it is all melted, Half a Quarter of a Pint of Water is ſufficient; then take an Ounce and Half of Stone-Blue diſſolv'd in a little Water, put it to the Gumboodge when melted; put to it a Quarter of a Pound of fine Sugar, and a Quarter of a Pint of Water more, and let it boil: Put a Spoonful of this to a Pint of any white Clear-Cakes, it will make them a very good Green.

To ſugar all Sorts of ſmall FRUIT.

BEAT the White of an Egg, and dip the Fruit in it; let it lye on a Cloth that it may not wet; then take fine ſifted Sugar, and rowl the Fruit in it 'till 'tis quite cover'd with

Sugar; lay it on a Sieve in a Stove, or before a Fire, to dry it well; it will keep well a Week.

To ſcald all Sorts of FRUIT.

PUT the Fruit into ſcalding Water, (as much as will almoſt cover the Fruit) ſet it over a ſlow Fire, keep them in a Scald 'till they are tender, turning the Fruit where the Water does not cover it; when 'tis very tender, lay a Paper cloſe to it, and let it ſtand 'till it is cold: Then to a Pound of Fruit put Half a Pound of Sugar, and let it boil (but not too faſt) 'till it looks clear: All Fruit muſt be done whole but Pippins, and they are beſt halv'd or quarter'd, and a little Orange-Peel boil'd and put in them, with the Juice of a Lemmon.

FINIS.